TERRY GILLIAM'S

FEAR AND LOATING IN LAS VEGAS

THE UNTOLD STORY

MONASTRELL BOOKS
2014

INTRA-COASTAL: ONE YEAR ON ST. PETE
BEACH (VOLUME ONE)
© 2014 by Justin Gene Gregorits

INTRA-COASTAL: ONE YEAR ON ST PETE
BEACH Volume One is a work of fiction. Any
resemblance of characters in this work to people
dead, or soon to be dead, is entirely coincidental.

First published as Monastrell 015 in October 2014.

Manufactured in the United States of America.

All Monastrell titles are published for Monastrell
Books by Gene Gregorits.

www.monastrellbooks.com

FIRST PRINTING, October 2014.

Introduction: © 2014 Gene Gregorits
Book design: Gene Gregorits

INTRODUCTION

GENE GREGORITS

Terry Gilliam's *Fear and Loathing In Las Vegas* was released in November of 1998, and tanked at the box office. The most venemous and politically extreme movie to be released by a major studio in years, its ferocious drug abuse angered many a critic and forced television networks to refuse commercial airtime to Universal Pictures. The following year, the 20th Century Fox release *Fight Club*, directed by David Fincher, once again had both conservatives and liberals up in arms. (Reportedly, it prompted the firing of studio employee Art Linson, director of the 1980 Hunter Thompson film *Where the Buffalo Roam*.)

In the late 90s, drugs, dissent, and a general sense of unrest were more absent than ever in the world of big-budget entertainment. Fincher's film was a malicious bastard, loaded to the gills on a cocktail of testosterone and slacker cynicism, while Gilliam's rose out of the 60's acid hangover, post-Vietnam guilt, and the dangerous hedonism of an era which the film's young target audience had never experienced first hand. *Fear and Loathing*'s ghoulishly surreal indictment of American greed and excess was a precise re-creation of Hunter S. Thompson's novel, making almost no concessions to the pre-millenial zeitgeist. The production and release of *Fear and Loathing* was indeed an abnormal and almost unbelievable actuality, too uncompromised to be anything other than a labor of love. Laila Nabulsi, the film's producer, knows the grueling tale like no other.

Sexiness, compassion, integrity, devotion...not a list of qualities you could expect from a Hollywood film producer. No one this side of Idi Amin has a repuation more deservedly putrid than the wheeling, dealing demons of Tinseltown's production offices. With such people in mind, Los Angeles can be seen only as an apocalyptic slaughterhouse, a quagmire of incest and cannibalism. A joyless Bacchanalia of greedy shitheads, caring for nothing more than sex orgies and their next million. Only those with the blackest hearts and psychotically fevered egos can survive there, it would seem...but Laila Nabulsi endures the sickness. And it's a miracle, really...a sign of supernatural strength, steel nerves, true bravado. It took all that and more to reach the other side of the *Fear and Loathing* tunnel. You have to admire the hell out of her for it.

Anyone with a fondness for Terry Gilliam's 1998 adaptation, considered by NY critic J. Hoberman to be "the most expensive midnight movie ever made", should know the full history, and to the best of my knowledge, Laila told it to a journalist in its episodic entirety only once, on a sunny afternoon in my Los Angeles living room. Since then, I've received requests from fanzines, magazines, and anthologies to run the piece. My answer was, invariably, "print everything, all 40 pages, or forget it." It's probably the most historically rich interview I've ever done, and says most if not all of what needs to be said about what Hollywood has come to represent. If you ever wondered about the cold-blooded grotesquerie one encounters when a work of such freak-power magnitude is optioned for commercial adaptation 25 years after its publication, you have an abundance of answers here (even though this is but a mere sampling of the original text).

Hunter Thompson created a new folk mythology when he decided to use two symbols of suicidal excess, Las Vegas and himself, as portals to a truer understanding of the capitalist nightmare which everything and everyone he saw was drowning in. That merciless, stomach-churning, and heartbreakingly poetic post-mortem called *Fear and Loathing in Las Vegas* took his obsession with the death of the American dream, begun with *Hell's Angels* in 1966, to its furthest logical extremity. *Fear and Loathing* officially launched that obsession as one which was to emerge as a permanent theme for Thompson. His fear of America's stupidity, his loathing of its selfishness and banality, would come to define the man until the end of his life. Thompson was that special breed of educated miscreant whose insolence was justified through his own magic talent of articulation in both word and in deed. He charged the very air around him with demonic brilliance, a reflective energy so powerful that it drowned out all noise but his own.

In *Fear and Loathing*, Thompson and friend Oscar Zeta Acosta's bizarrely poignant rampage through Sin City was truthfully portrayed by the author; an extended, drug-swamp session of Russian Roulette, in which he used himself simultaneously as social thermometer and toxically insane guinea pig...a method that was at once romantic, utilitarian, and miserably pathetic. When the storm finally broke, through the cirrocumulous clouds of Thompson's over-stimulated brainmeat, a vision of Hell began to form. That vision has never left us, and the superhuman commitment of Laila Nabulsi, a woman who deeply loved and understood this violent man named Thompson, has in no small way served to further embolden a work which continues to penetrate untold thousands of virgin minds with each passing year.

FEAR AND LOATHING IN HOLLYWOOD

Being the TRUE, MOSTLY UNCENSORED Tale of GREED, ARROGANCE, FOUL PLAY, and METHOD CIGARETTE BURNS, Featuring the Misadventures of One Miss **LAILA NABULSI** In Her 20 Year Courtship of "THE FILM"; an Endless Saga to the BLACK, VIRULENT HEART of the American Gonzo Film Adapation NIGHTMARE and Beyond

GENE GREGORITS: Say, "Horrible".
LAILA NABULSI: "HORRIBLE!"
GG: That's good. I think this is working.
LN: And I can sit over there.
GG: I can get a chair…

LYDIA LUNCH: No. Both of you. Over there.

LN: We both sit over there?

LL: Yes.

TAPE CUTS

GG: When was the film adapation of Fear & Loathing first discussed?

LL: And also, my question is, why did it take thirty years?

LN: Not enough sex, too much guts. (laughs) Okay. I'll try to make it a simple story, simply told. There was a guy in London, named Lou Stein. Hunter and I were in Mobile, hiding out, and Hunter was supposed to be writing something, and I was trying to get a driver's license-

GG: What year is this?

LN: Eighty-one, maybe? So we were living in a friend's condo, in Mobile. Going to IHOP for breakfast, things like that. Some guy from England called, out of the blue, named Lou Stein. Very nervously, he said he had not only *written* a play of *Fear & Loathing In Las Vegas*, but it was about to go on, in London. He had neglected to get the rights to do it. So he was now calling at the last hour. Being the gatekeeper that I was, I said, *"Well,* I have no idea who you are."* He had done some other plays so I said "send me some reviews of your other plays". He sent me the reviews. He'd done some adaptations. He'd done *Day Of The Locust*, and things like that. And they were all good reviews. I thought, "this sounds pretty great." I wondered, "how *could* he have adapted it?" It was sort of an interesting idea.

Hunter and I decided that we would go to London and see the play! The poor guy, I called him and said, "the good news is, you can do it. The bad news is, we're coming to see it when it opens." He was excited. We went to London, we went to see this play open. It was really great! And what he did, which is really smart...he used the device of a narrator, so there were two Hunters. There was the one on the stage doing the action, and the other was the narrator, who said all the [long passages] in the book, this sort of internal monologue, with natural breaks in the story. And the actors were all English actors, so it was kind of [strange]. But the guy who did Gonzo was really great, he did the bathtub scene, and he ran around naked onstage...

GG: (laughs)

LN: Lou Stein, it turned out, was actually a guy from Brooklyn who had an English accent because he'd been living there so long. My first thought was, "well, why don't I do the play in America, you know, as an American version? And then, *somebody* said, along the way, "why don't you just do the movie? Why don't you just find out what the rights are?" Hunter had theatrical rights, but he had sold the movie rights. So I had to chase these guys down. What happened was, in 1976, Hunter had sold the rights in perpetuity-

LL: Ehhhhh!

LN: -for ten thousand dollars, to John Jergens, who is the heir to the Jergens hand cream fortune.

GG: Hahahaha!

LN: He didn't know. He was a sweet guy, and doesn't have a clue. John Jergens had also gotten involved with this guy, *Shark Productions*, they called themselves. The other guy's name was Joe Bianco, in New York, who was a kind of New York, Wall Street shark, but a very Gonzo looking guy. Big, fat Italian guy, who was smart as a whip, but...*God knows* what was going on there. First I had to hunt them down. I had no idea where to find them. And that took a while. The thing was that Hunter had never *signed* the agreement. He had taken the money, so legally that is like signing an agreement, but he had never actually signed it. So, in a way, you could say that there wasn't really a clean chain of titles. I had *that* in my back pocket. So I found these guys, went to them, and I said "look, I'd like to produce the movie. You guys bought this in perpetuity for *no money*, that's not really fair. Hunter never signed the agreement....let's negotiate. Why don't you give it to me for seven years." At the time I thought, "well, seven years!" Big deal, right? "And then it will revert back to Hunter, which seems fair, or you need to pay more money. You need to pay Hunter more money." *And they went along with it*! So this guy John Jergens was basically my investment/development person. At the end of the day, he put in like $250,000. And he did get his money back, I *did* get it back to him. He was the kind of guy that would fly standby, himself, at times, but he was always building huge houses in Hawaii, or Taos.

I, meanwhile, was just wandering around, trying to figure out how to do this. The first thing I did was I got Lou Stein to write a first draft of the screenplay. We went to Vegas. Another guy involved in the Shark group was Frank Sinatra's stepson, Bobby Marx. So he got us the hotel rooms, and tickets to shows. We got to see Sammy Davis Jr. and Jerry Lewis, *and it was fun*! We got this first draft. And I didn't really like that first draft that much, it just didn't do anything for me. Ralph Steadman got it to Handmade films, which was George Harrison's company, and they loved it but they thought it was too wild. You've gotta remember, this was the 80's, the "Just Say No" Reagan-era. Everybody we brought it to just said *"No way, NO way."* I mean, "Ooooh, it's hysterical, but we could never do this."

In the meantime, Hunter and I had broken up. People always ask, "How did you get the rights to Fear and Loathing?" I always say, "it was cheaper than palimony." So, that was the one thing that I did have. So I went in and out of wanting to do it, not wanting to do it. It was hard. I was living in New York. I finally decided at some point that if I wanted to do it, I should come out to LA, and just concentrate. I made a decision at a certain point: "Okay, I'm going to MAKE THIS MOVIE." It was a weird cross to bear, like a fuckin' *monster* that wouldn't go away. I did talk to people. See, I could always *talk* to people about it because everybody knew the book. But people were so skittish over the material. And especially in the 80s. It wasn't until Gus Van Sant made *Drugstore Cowboy* that the ide of *Fear & Loathing* became more acceptable.

GG: Drugstore Cowboy, yeah.

LN: And what happened was, I was in LA and I was friends with this agent Stephen Starr ay William Morris. He called me, he said, you know, you should meet this guy Gus Van Sant. At this point Gus had *shot* Drugstore Cowboy. It hadn't come out yet. He sent me this film Gus had done, which was his first film. It was this *gay*...

LL: Malle Noche?

LN: Yeah. I mean, it *looked* great, but I was so freaked out because it was this weird gay thing and I'm thinking, Fear and Loathing? This guy? I don't know. I said, "okay, fine, I'll meet him, whatever. I met him at Cantors, we had a nice talk. He knew the book. He said that he would like to do the movie. And he wanted me to come see a early cut of Drugstore Cowboy that he was screening. I saw that, and said "OH! Great!" We're talking about *Fear & Loathing,* and *then* Drugstore Cowboy came out and it just turned into a huge hit for him. Then it started getting crazy, and everybody was on his case. They wanted him to do different movies, not another drug movie. It turned into that thing, which happens, when they get successful.

LL: Well, we see where it has led, with Gus Van Sant. BORING, MAINSTREAM, FEEL-GOOD POINTLESS DRIVEL...*Gus*.

LN: The truth is he's not a...

GG: Hahaha! Sorry Gus.

LL: Don't apologize to him.

LN: ...I don't think he's a screenwriter, really. I mean, he tried to do that...what was that movie he did, the adaptation?

GG: Even Cowgirls Get The Blues. Heard it was AWFUL!

LN: *WOW*...

GG: That bad?

LN: Really bad. But, thing is, he definitely has the visual chops, and I *liked* him when I met him. I had *no idea* he was gay. Even when I met him. And I asked him, you know, "why did you pick a gay subject for Malle Noche?" He said, "well, when you're going to do a short film, a student kind of thing, people usually do horror films, and I wanted to do something different, that would shock people." I said, "well, I *guess you did*." I like that movie he did with River Phoenix...

LL: My Own Private Idaho.

LN: When he called me to say that he wouldn't be doing *Fear & Loathing,* he sounded a little *stressed*. He said, "look. They want me to do these big movies, and I'm just gonna go do My Own Private Idaho." I was diasppointed, but I respected his choice to do an independent project.

GG: So we're into the early 90's here...

LN: Early 90s. When did Drugstore Cowboy come out?

GG: Like 88, 89. But you directed some plays during the second half of the 80s, during that time when you were putting Fear and Loathing on and off the shelf?

LN: I was working on films. I worked with Anjelica Houston, did Prizzi's Honor. I worked for the producer John Foreman, who I consider to be my mentor. I went *back* to Saturday Night Live in 1985, and got a new cast. The year Lorne Michaels went back. He asked me to come back and find a new cast, to be the associate producer to run the show and hire the hosts...

GG: Let's backtrack here. Rewind. I'm curious what you did prior to to SNL, your first stint there. What was your first SNL experience?

LN: I went to high school at the United Nations International School. My best friend there was Elissa Guest. Her brother was Christopher Guest. I met Chris when I was about 16. *He* was in a show called *Lemmings*.

GG: (chuckles)

LN: *Lemmings* was a stage show. Chevy Chase was in it. Belushi was in it. He just came in from Chicago. It was a rock'n'roll parody show. Chris did Bob Dylan. Belushi did Joe Cocker. It was a really great show, a little show, in New York. And I remember going to see that show. And then, there was something called the National Lampoon Radio Hour. Chris Guest helped start it. Right after high school, I hitchhiked through Europe with my friend Alyssa. Then I spent a year in England, where I attended an American college for one year. When I returned to the States, I decided I wanted to be an actress. I attended acting school for a year. Then I hanging out at National Lampoon Radio Hour. Chris Guest was my boyfriend at that time, even though he made me extremely nervous.

GG: (laughs)

LN: So, I was hanging around there, and Belushi was there along with a lot of the people who started the Lampoon. Doug Kenney, he was a good friend of mine. He was a great guy. So there was this whole crowd. Michael O'Donohough was a writer there. What I say now is that comedy was my real college. There was a group of actors, a group of performers, a group of writers, a group *people* that were hanging out together. This was around 1974 or 1975.

TAPE CUTS

LN: I met Bill Murray the first day he came to New York. They brought him in from Chicago, where he had been in Second City. Belushi knew him there. They brought him in to do something on the radio hour. The second day he was there, he and I ran all over the city. I remember now, it was *pouring rain*. And he was *so* funny. He made me laugh *all day long*. We went down to Wall Street and we went to the Stock Exchange. And I tease him now, I say, "remember when you used to be really funny?" He was really wild, and in fact, *everybody* just went all the way out there with everything they had. And he was the comic poetic genius. He could riff on *anything*. He could be sitting here now making us laugh about what we're doing, right now. You might not even remember it, but you would be on the floor, hysterical. All those guys were around and they did another show, a *stage* show, called "The Lampoon Show". It was Harold Ramis, Bill Murray, his brother Brian Murray, and Gilda Radner. She had just come from Second City in Toronto. Belushi was in it too. We were all friends, and I became best friends with Belushi. I broke up with Chris Guest, and it was a terrible, horrible hearbreak for me. I was really young. Belushi was the one that kind of got me out of that, by being my friend. Anyway, that was our crowd. We'd hang out and go to breakfast together. Nobody had a lot of money, and we were just hanging out. Then Saturday Night Live happened and a lot of these people got on the show. The National Lampoon group basically transferred to the show. Writers and performers. There were lots of Second City people. Suddenly there was this *bigger* forum for what was already going on. I could have just hung out and had a good time, but I really wanted to *do* something. Tom Schiller was there and he was starting to make these short films. Belushi said to him, "why don't you let Laila work with you?" So Tom and I became partners in crime, and we did a lot of short films for the show.

GG: What *kind* of short films?

LN: I should have brought you the tape. I forgot about that. A lot of them were black and white. *Schiller's Reel*, it was called. We did one with Belushi called "Don't Look Back In Anger", where he's an old man in the graveyard. It is the Not Ready For Prime Time Players cemetary. And everybody's dead except him. Isn't that ironic? Then we had La Dolce Gilda, where we did a Fellini parody with Gilda. We actually won *some* award, for one we did called Java Junkie, which was a takeoff on *The Lost Weekend*, about a guy who's addicted to caffiene.

GG: Hahaha.

LN: It was a three minute film. Very stylized.

LL: And that was made for Saturday Night Live.

LN: Yeah, it was aired. But it was a great education for me because we were just making these films like renegades. We had one camera and we would just run around the streets and made them for no money.

LL: And it was wide open then!

LN: It was wide open! We had our own small group of actors that we liked to use in our movies, and we had, obviously, the SNL cast. So we had *those* guys. We'd run around and we'd *make things up* sometimes! Tom made one up one day called "Picasso: The New York Years". Picasso was never *in* New York! So we ran around New York, and we interviewed people in deli's, for example. "Oh Picasso used to come in here. He bought this meat!" It was fun. And I learned how to work with no budget, and I learned how to get releases, and find out where the film goes. But the great thing about it was, creatively, that in all that messing around, we *had* an audience! Suddenly, it's *on TV*, in a big way, and you're getting a response! People are laughing and they're getting it. It was like being at some kind of college, with the added benefit of this: you actually had to do the work. And *plus*, there was an incredible hubris of all those great people. You always had somebody to bounce off of!

LL: It was so spontaneous, as opposed to now.

LN: It really spoiled me! First of all, I *love* groups of people. I work really well with groups. I love the idea of having a *community* that you can bounce off of. Now that doesn't mean that everybody got along with everybody else all the time, but you could go into somebody's office at any time and go "what do you think of this?" Constant comedy *repartee* going on. Also, you had a very *fast* in-and-out! You're coming up with an idea, it's on TV, and before you know it, you're on to the next thing.

LL: The faster you create, the faster you *can* create.

LN: You're not *waiting around*. Of course, you're talking about a lot of performers, and so there's also the heartbreak of a great scene getting cut at the last minute.

LL; So who *didn't* get along?

LN: (laughs) Well, Chevy was pretty reviled.

GG: Yeah, a lot of people don't like him.

LL: Is he smug?

LN: Well, he *left*, you know. He left by the second year. He didn't stay long. He was the first one to break out. The first one to leave, to go to Hollywood or whatever he was doing. To get married or whatever. But he and John never got along. They *hated* each other.

LL: Well, one was as loose as a person can get, and the other one seemed uptight from the get go anyway.

LN: Well, you have to look at it ethnically. Here's Chevy, this white Americana god of money and...

GG: He reminds me of a smartass Mercedes Benz salesman.

LL: Hahaha!

LN: Wellll...Chevy was everything that John didn't come from. Here's John, first generation Albanian. Struggling. And *then*, here's this guy who seems to have it all or come from it all.

LL: Wasn't alcohol a divide too, at that point?

LN: Well, *everybody* was doing drugs and alcohol. I'll tell you something about Chevy. Chevy is *very funny*, and he's very smart. But he's got that kind of sense of humor where he'll *go for the joke*, no matter what. One of the first times I ever met Chevy, I left the room in tears! He made some joke at my expense, and I don't even remember what it was. I'm sure he doesn't either. But I realized then, if you can't take the heat get out of the kitchen. If you can't hang with the guys, and take that kind of comedy, take a hike. And I'm a perfect target. I was so *trusting*, and I believed things people said. I was the perfect setup at times.

LL: (laughs)

LN: But then I realized that I just couldn't let them get to me like that. That's just the deal. Chevy would say things to John like, "Did you shave your back today?"

GG: (laughs)

LN: Shit like that. But it was *rough*, and it was a very male-dominated environment. The girls tried to stick together. All the female writers like my friend Anne Beatts, and Marilyn Miller. Those girls really had it tough. And they had to battle constantly to get their comedy in there because the guys were really strong! But sometimes I think comedy is very male-oriented anyway. But it never bothered me because Schiller was very collaborative. And we had our own little thing with the film department. And John was my best friend and protector, so I didn't *have* to go fight with Lorne Michaels or fight the guys, really. That came later, in 1985, when I went to graduate school with Loren.

GG: Was it usually Aykroyd and Belushi holding court at the bar, or whever the gang would hang out?

LN: Belushi was, I would say, the warm center of the group. He was a very embracing personality. He loved to hang out. People would be at his house all the time. He and Danny were very close. I remember the first time I met Danny. The first time Saturday Night Live was really going to happen, Belushi had a party at his place on Bleecker Street. He had this one bedroom apartment. All these people came over. We were all there. Danny was there. Schiller was there. That was the first time I met Schiller too. We'd been having these parties with the Lampoon group, and *now* we were having these *new* parties, with a *new* kind of group. That was the beginning. I was still with Chris Guest, I think. I remember going to the party with Chris and Chris was upset because he didn't *get on the show*. That was really hard. There were people who were part of the group who didn't get picked up. He did do the show later. I was sitting in the living room and Danny was sitting next to me. We just started holding hands. We had this immediate affinity. (laughs) And I look up and there's my boyfriend and I'm like *what is this*? It wasn't necessarily a pick up, it was just "oh! You're here." There was a lot of that feeling of…what Vonnegut calls a *karass*, you know? It was like a bunch of souls that had come together to do this thing. There was a lot of everybody figuring out who everybody else was. There were *natural affinities* and groups. There was John, John's wife Judy, myself and Danny. There was *that* contingent. Then there was the Lorne contingent, of Lorne, Chevy, and a few others.

GG: Saturday Night Live, for a while, has had this tradition of huge after-show parties, where they wrap up, go out, and sometimes have to make false reservations to trick the crowds and the sycophants. Was it like that then too?

LN: Oh yeah. We used to go to this place called One Fifth, on Fifth Avenue. For a while, that was the big one. We had *lots* of after-parties there. And what happened was, Danny got the Blues Bar, which was just a hole in the wall. It was a bar, and they bought it. It was our secret after-hours place. And we would go from the party to the Blues Bar.

LL: Where was that?

LN: It was downtown. In those days, Tribeca was *no-mans-land*. It was right in that area. Now it's probably a street that has galleries, and shops. Danny would know. I can't remember. The funny thing is, we would just grab musicans and guest hosts from the show and take them there. See, *everyone* would come to the show! All the talent of the day wanted to be at SNL, so we met *everybidy*, which was the most fun thing about it. Then we would grab these famous people and drag them down to the Blues Bar. Sometimes we had instruments and we'd make these people play them. John would make them play with him. John had a band and it was called the Stinkband because they were just atrocious. I remember one time when I looked up and there was Bowie playing keyboards with the Stinkband. Somebody came up to me and said, "who's that guy, he's really *terrible*!"

LL: Hahahahaha!

GG: That makes me feel good.

LN: They didn't realize it was Bowie! I was like, "yeah but he's playing with the Stinkband, what do you expect?" But yeah, you got to meet everybody who you thought you ever wanted to meet. Which was *great* and it was fun! But being so young and owning the city in that way was memorable. Some people say they regret their youth, that they shouldn't have done the things they did. I can't say that. I feel that, at least in my youth, I had the experience of having as much fun as I could possibly have.

LL: And surviving it.

GG: (grumbling)

LN: And *surviving* it, yeah! Because it was like a war. I remember I was at a party once and I heard someone say, "I was in Viet Nam" and another guy said "I was at Saturday Night Live." It was like that too.

LL: So how did you meet Hunter and why did you run off with him?

LN: I met Hunter in John Belushi's dressing room. What happened was, the summer before John and Danny had gone on a road trip for Rolling Stone Magazine. And Judy Belushi and I, we ran around and we got the car, we got the supplies they needed. And at one point, I remember saying to Judy, "why are we doing this? Why don't *we* go on the fucking road trip?" So they went off on this road trip and they stopped is Aspen Colorado and met Hunter. I had a vague idea of **Fear & Loathing**. I think that came out in... '71?

GG: Yeah.

LN: I may have even read it, but I didn't have a real focus on it. The guys' trip was in 1976. They came back talking about this guy Hunter Thompson, and I knew he was from the South, but I didn't pay attention because there was always so much going on. One Saturday night, before the show I got a call from Belushi. He called that night and said, "Go to my house! I need this jacket for the show. And come right down!" So I go down there, and walk into his dressing room, and there's this guy lying on the couch. This *long* looking person with shorts on, and sneakers. This *face*.

GG: (breaking into hysterical laughter)

LN: The night I met Hunter, it was like a bomb dropped, okay? Now let me tell you something: you could walk into anybody's dressing room, especially John's, at any time during those years, and it could be *anybody*. It could be a dealer. A messenger. It could be Frank Sinatra. It could be anybody. I didn't know who *this* was, because I'd never seen him before. And in my mind, I thought Hunter Thompson would look like Truman Capote writing. Because he was Southern. I don't know. There was no other image in my mind. This bomb has now dropped and I remember thinking, "oh my god, who is this person? What is this, what is this? I'm either going to love this person, or hate this person." There was all this energy. I stand there and I give John the jacket, and John goes, "Oh!" And he loved to do this, he loved to introduce me to people. One of my favorite memories was when we were at this club and he was yelling at me across the room, "Laila! Laila!" He was standing next to this strange guy with a tan. I walk over and he goes, "LAILA? *FABIAN!*"

LL: (laughing)

LN: So it was that kind of a thing, right? So...back to the dressing room. Belushi *says proudly*, "Oh! Laila Nabulsi, *HUNTER THOMPSON.* Hunter Thompson, *LAILA NABULSI.*" And in that moment I thought, "oh no, you brought all *that stuff* with you?" Like a past life kind of thing, whatever "that" is. As if I already knew what "that stuff" was, even though I had no idea what "it" was. I couldn't look at him and I couldn't really focus on what he looked like. So anyway, the show's going to start. Hunter doesn't want to go sit in his seat, he wants to stay in the dressing room. John says, "*you* stay here with him, and make sure he's okay." I used to walk around a lot during the show, and check things out. So I did that. I would go and come back, you know, to check on Hunter. John would run in every so often, then run out. We were watching the show on this tiny little monitor. At one point, Hunter went into the bathroom. It was a *tiny* room. And he *looked* weird! There was something wrong with him. He came out of the bathroom and I said something to him like, "are you alright?" And he looks up, sharply, and says, "I WAS WEEPING IN THERE."

GG /LL: (laughing)

LN: And I *believed* him! See, because I believed everything anybody said. And I didn't know what his sense of humor was like! I thought, "OH MY GOD! He's crying? Why is he crying?" And then I remember being at the party, afterwards. He was sitting with some people and I was sitting far away from him and he kept looking at me. I could just see his face through the fog, the smoke, with his cigarette holder. And I was like, "*what IS that*?"

LL: (laughing)

LN: John came up to me at the party, with the eyebrow up and the whole charm thing going, and he says, "Listen. I just have to go someplace. But Hunter needs to go back to my apartment and I'm going to give him the limo. But I need you to go with him and make sure he gets back into the apartment." This whole rigamarole to get me to go *with him*, in the limo, to the apartment. "Here are the keys." I look at John and I said, "Alright. But I'm not gonna fuck him."

LL; (laughs)

LN: John started laughing. Well, what I *didn't* know, which I found out later, was that he had gone to Hunter with this whole scenario of "I have to go somewhere and then I'll meet you back there." He said to Hunter, here are the keys but *what do you need*?" Hunter had appraently pointed to me and said "HER." So John had to come and convince me to go with him! It was surprising, because John was my protector. He was my big brother. He *never* let anyone get near me! So, he must have really needed to go wherever he was going. Hunter and I get in the limo, go down to John's apartment, we get into the apartment, set down on the couch and after about thirty seconds, Hunter *LEAPS* across the couch on top of me.

[Everyone laughs]

LN: I'm thinking "what the FUCK is this?" The entire episode was so terrifying. And there's a tangle of clothes, right? And then, suddenly, BUZZ BUZZ BUZZ!, the doorbell is ringing insistently. John had obviously re-thought leaving us alone.

LL: Great!

LN: He saved the day. Quickly, the clothes were put back on. Nothing happened. John comes up. I tell him, "you left me with a monster." I ended up falling asleep on the couch. It's by now six in the morning. I'm trying to sleep and I can hear them laughing, and laughing and laughing. Laughing and talking all night long. Then, John's wife Judy, who had been out of town, got back in around 7 a.m. It was the end of the evening. I'm getting up to leave, and Hunter says, "DON'T LEAVE WITHOUT ME."

LL: (laughs)

LN: And *where* am I supposed to take *him*? (laughing) Waaaaait a minute! I lived around the corner. So somehow, despite John's protests, we leave together. I said to Hunter, "Well…I'm going home." And he says, "I'M COMING WITH YOU." So suddenly he comes over to my house. Crazy. I had this one room apartment, a studio apartment. I had been given these parakeets which were tortured at the Lampoon Radio Hour for sound effects. These parakeets. I had taken them home with me but they had gotten out of the cage and I could never get them back inside. So they basically lived in the biggest birdcage in New York, my apartment. They were always flying around. So now Hunter and I are back to my place. We got busy. (laughs) We were fine until he said something to me like, "You know I'm going to have to *kill you*." You know, one of his things that he says to be funny. But I *believed* him! I thought, "OH NOW HE'S GOING TO KILL ME!" So I tried to throw him out of the apartment, screaming "you've gotta get THE FUCK OUT OF HERE!"

GG: (laughing)

LN: And he just wasn't going anywhere! By now it is Sunday, and I had to go meet some friend of my Dad's at the Plaza Hotel for lunch, some kind of insane diplomatic thing. I left Hunter in my apartment! He just wouldn't leave. So I said, "okay, well...DON'T LOOK AT MY STUFF!" (laughs) I left him there and he ended up staying in town for two weeks at the Gramercy Park Hotel. And I ended up staying there with him a lot. It was crazy. I didn't find out until about a week and a half into it that he was married. When I found that out, I freaked. Then I found that out, and I freaked out. I backed off from him. He got back with his wife. Then they finally broke up, and...you know. We ran back into each other and it all started up again. But...that's how we met.

GG: That's a great story. (long pause) Lydia, help me! What's next?

TAPE CUTS

GG: Okay, so what we do now is, we skip ahead to...well, no. Hmmm. I guess then that we should talk about the Curse of Lono.

LN: (groans)

GG: Okay, then that's out. Flash forward...the movie! You left off with Gus Van Sant dropping out, circa 1990.

LN: Gus Van Sant dropped out. And I talked with everyone, every writer, every producer, every director.

LL: In the beginning of trying to get this developed, before Johnny Depp came into the picture, who did you have in mind, or *did you* have any stars in mind? Was Johnny Depp a Johnny Come Lately?

LN: Jack Nicholson and Marlon Brando.

LL: Hahaha!

LN: Thank *god* it wasn't.

GG: Hey, that would have been amazing!

LN: They would have been great! I have to say that Jack was certainly great to me, because when I was first beginning production on the movie, I went to Jack and he gave me notes on how to do the movie. When it was in development. He sat with me for three hours, and we talked about the movie. He actually said to me at one point, "are you going to direct it?" Which was probably what I should have done, in the long run, if I'd had it together, if I'd had any clout to do it. Because I really *did* know it so well. I knew what I wanted it to be. The other great advice he gave me was this. I told him, "I don't know how to do this" or "I don't know how to do that." He said, "just do what you like doing. You can always find somebody else to do the other stuff." Which was the *best advice*, because I realized, what I was good at, I was able to do and keep it going. I did *send* the book to Marlon Brando. I sent it to the Coen Brothers at one point. I sent it to any person who I thought was the right type for the material. I even gave the book to Gregg Araki. I didn't even *know* Gregg Araki.

LL: (laughing)

GG: Oh GOD!

LN: I didn't even know what kind of movies that he made, but somebody talked me into it. I went to his apartment-

GG: (moaning in sheer agony)

LN: -he opened the door, and here was this weird guy. I gave him the book **Fear & Loathing**. He closed the door and I never heard from him again. (hysterical laughter)

GG: Gregg Araki is our number one enemy.

LN: Is he?

GG: Yes, because he may indeed be the most repulsive human being alive on the face of this planet today.

LN: Well, you know, the thing about the Gregg Araki story was, at one point during the whole shenanigans of actually getting the movie made, some agent *accused me* of going behind Alex Cox's back, when Cox was doing the film and offering it to Gregg Araki. Which is ridiculous because I'd never heard back from him.

LL: Oh JESUS! Alex COX? So you went from sewer to sewer, from Araki to Cox?

GG: How the hell can you say that? Cox is amazing! Haven't you seen *Straight To Hell*? It's one of the funniest movies ever made.

LL: *Pfffffffft.*

LN: Oh please. Cox is an assh-

LL: He is the WORST.

GG: It goes over some people's heads I guess.

LN: He's the WORST! And he is the *biggest fucking asshole* on the planet.

LL: Cox is truly the worst alive.

GG: Yeah, yeah. Let's move on.

LL: Gene loves his lousy films.

GG: They're funny.

LN: *Sid & Nancy, Repo Man*…okay.

GG: I hated *Sid & Nancy*.

LN: Since then, crap. But I'm not here to judge the man on his creative merits!

LL: I AM!

LN: On a personal level, he's impossible. It's so hard when you do interviews, because you think, "*well*, I might want to work with that person again." But what I'm saying is, I would *crawl*...down the boulevard, *on broken glass*...before I would even think about sitting in the same *room* with Alex Cox again.

TAPE CUTS

GG: Alex Cox wrote the screenplay-

LN: NO HE DIDN'T!

GG: -which Terry Gilliam then *re-wrote*-

LN: No, he did *not* write the screenplay!

GG: I thought Terry Gilliam re-wrote Cox's screenplay...

LN: Alex wrote *a version* of the screenplay, which nobody wanted to do!

GG: Well, how is is different than the final version?

LN: First of all, when you have a book that's pretty much what the film is, *anybody* can write an adaptation of that book, and they're gonna *use the same shit*. No basically, he used the same shit, that everybody else had done, that *I had already done*. I had already done two versions of the screenplay, and I *told* him, this is how it goes. "This is what it is." Okay?

GG: Yes.

LN: *Now*...he decided he was going to go off and write a screenplay. So he goes off. He comes back, and there were a couple of things...certainly, that were his *own* taste. There were a couple of details that were glaringly inappropriate, things that I just couldn't accept. One was *the wave speech*. "We were riding the crest of a high and beautiful wave." That was the *soul* of the book.

GG: Well, YEAH! It's the soul of the film, too.

LN: It's the soul of the film too. Then there's a speech we have at the end, in which Tim Leary is mentioned, and he talks about the *grim meathook realities*.

TAPE CUTS

GG: We're rolling.

LN: Okay, so Alex Cox put the two speeches together and more or less *bastardized* the wave speech…which was a real problem for me, and actually for Johnny and everybody else. We were all sort of like, "*what*?" And then he had an *animated sequence*.

GG: Was Johnny attached from the beginning of pre-production?

LN: Well, at this point Johnny was attached. I met with Alex a few years before. He came and took a meeting with me at Rhino, when I was first dealing with Rhino. This was *after* my deal with Ridley Scott's company. I was going to make the movie with *Jake* Scott, Ridley's son. We worked on the script for a year, we worked on the script. And then Ridley's company lost their financing and the whole thing fell apart. Jake didn't want to do *Fear & Loathing* at that point and I was back to owning it, and not having anything. Rhino had been knocking at the back door saying "*we* wanna do it!" I thought, "well, I'd rather be a bigger fish in a small pond, than a small fish in a big pond." It was kind of a bad idea, because Rhino didn't have enough experience to know what they were doing. They just ran amok for a while. During that time, I did meet with Alex Cox, as I was meeting with other people. He went to a meeting at Rhino with me. Well...*he didn't do his homework* before the meeting! He hadn't read the book, he didn't really know what was going on. He wasn't very good in the meeting. And I just thought, "forget it." I wasn't interested. Things are still rolling along, I'm still looking for the right director. Then I went around the block with Lee Tamahori, who had just done...

GG: *Once Were Warriors*.

LN: Yeah, *Once Were Warriors*. I went after him. And he was really into it. He actually went with me to meet with Hunter. Again, like with Gus Van Sant, he was in that situation that happens to a lot of people when they come here and they start getting successful or when they're on the cusp of getting successful, they want to do those big Hollywood movies, and they want the payday. They get all these other offers. *Fear & Loathing*...is *hard*! It scared a lot of people, and I think we just couldn't get them to deal with what it took to commit to it. So Tamahori was holding me up, and Rhino was facing deadlines with their option agreements. So they just went ahead and said "let's do it with Alex Cox", and they hired Alex Cox without me saying okay.

GG: Rhino is a strange company to begin with, and Alex Cox is borderline psychotic...

LN: Well, Rhino...they're *gleaners*. They find things that are already there and then they repackage them. I wouldn't call them creative geniuses. But they're good...in their own business.

GG: They're a reperatory company...

LN: (out of mic range)

GG: Ha ha.

LN: At the time, they weren't very saavy in the movie business.

GG: Rhino Films had just started.

LN: Rhino Films had just started and Steve Nemeth thought *Fear & Loathing* would be his ticket to becoming a player in Hollywood. He was running all over the place shooting his mouth off. So it was *really* difficult. Anyway, he just decided to hire Alex Cox and I said, "*waaaait* a minute!" But they had to hire *somebody* to make the option deadline. At the time I was still trying to get Johnny Depp to commit. Hunter was the one who came up with the idea, who said, "what about Johnny Depp?" He had met Johnny. I thought that if I had Johnny, it would change everything, that we could actually make this movie the right way. Now I've got Cox, who I don't want, but I'm *trying* to work with him. I'm trying to convince myself that he can do it. He ran off to do the script, which I already told you about. See, here's Alex Cox's big mistake: he decided to make *me* the *enemy*. The one person who has been the keeper of the flame, who's tied to Hunter, who's been doing it all along....and he decides that *I'm* the enemy. And that he's going to allign himself with Rhino...and with anybody else. But not me. And now he starts to treat me that way. And now he starts to fuck with my head that way.

GG: He's a bit of a misogynist, isn't he, that Alex?

LN: He's a *total* misogynist.

GG: Heh, heh, heh.

LL: An alcoholic?

LN: I don't know. There's something *wrong* with him. He's...

LL: Semi-retarded and illiterate?

GG: Hey, that's slander. Cox is brilliant.

LL: Pffffft.

LN: He's actually very bright, but he is *so* self-destructive. I've never seen anyone fuck himself over so badly. Because he *had it*. He *had* the opportunity and he BLEW IT. See, Alex challenged me, to the point where I couldn't take it. I'll tell you, quite honestly, there was a day when they had a casting session, and I showed up to come and sit in on the casting session...*and he didn't want me there*. I came in and I said, "look, I don't know what your problem is." And he actually stood there, and said to me *with venom-*

GG: Heh, heh, heh.

LN: *-venom and HATE* coming at me, and he said to me, "why don't you just let Rhino *buy you out*, and go away?" And I said, "you know what, Alex? That's not going to happen. So just...*get over it*." And he said, "*You're living in a FANTASY WORLD!*"

[GG & LL in hysterics.]

LN: Which of course, I *loved*. So we had this huge fight, and it was like the third time he'd fucked with me. The other times I hadn't reacted. I kept my cool, said, "okaaaay, I'm *trying*." This time, we had a *huuuuge* fight. Then he walked into the casting meeting. I got in my car and drove to Rhino's offices. I was actually crying, and was upset that he had actually gotten to me. Because he was SO vicious. I then got a flat tire and crashed my car into the curb. I went up to Steve Nemeth's office, saying, "you have *got* to get rid of him. I can't work with him. I WILL NOT work with him, not when he treats me this way. This is *my project*. Why the fuck do I have to deal with *this* asshole?" And blah, blah, blah. So Steve goes, "let's just try to get Johnny attached." That's when I realized that I had *nobody* on my side, and that if I didn't have someone *like* Johnny, who was on my team, and Hunter's team, that I was *fucked*! The challenge was there. I said, "okay, we'll see who wins." My attitude was, "you're gonna fuck with me? Okay. May the best man win."

LL: (chuckles)

LN: So meanwhile, I'm talking to Hunter. I'm not even *telling* Hunter how bad it is, because I'm afraid that we're gonna be stuck with Alex, and that everybody's gonna have to work with him. I fought to keep everybody okay with it. If I get Johnny to commit, we're still stuck with Alex, so I don't want anyone thinking that this is a disaster, you know?

GG: Yeah.

LN: And at this point, what was the last film that Cox had done?

LN: *Oh,* and that was the other thing! He showed us a tape of the last film he'd done, in Mexico. It was un*watchable*!

GG: Was it *Highway Patrolman*? That film…people either really love or really hate.

LL: I'm sure…I would hate it. I don't have to see it.

LN: I don't think it was *Highway Patrolman*, I think it was something else.

[Gene begins to babble about the films of Alex Cox, while Laila goes into further detail about the degree to which she hated the film in question.]

LN: …but anyway. We had one of those moments, where we were all at the screening, and I just said to myself, "we are in so much fuckin trouble."

LL: (laughs)

GG: Well whatever film it is, it apparently hasn't been released.

LL: Well, how does someone with each successive film get worse and worse and worse?

LN: Well, *again*…Alex is not stupid, he's very, very smart. I was *willing,* I was willing to try. He just decided, personally, to go after me. And he was *so* vicious that ultimately, I was left with no choice but to defend myself in some way.

LL: So you buddied up with Johnny-boy?

LN: Well, what happened was-

LL: Who wouldn't?

LN: What happened was, Hunter was being given the keys to the city, in Louisville. I knew Johnny was going, and Hunter invited me. So I went down there. Johnny was there, and Hunter was there, and I said, "listen, guys." The option was running *out*! That's why Rhino was running into total darkness, screaming, "we gotta make this! We gotta make this! And we've gotta start shooting before January!" We're in September at this point. And they're acting like *it's happening*. "It's all *happening*!" And I'm watching this, saying to myself, "oooooh, I'm in HELL, right now!" I don't have Johnny at this point, I don't have *anything*, except *Alex*.

LL: Hahaha.

LN: Obviously, no one is listening to me, no one gives a *shit* what I think. Hunter and Johnny agreed that we should just wait until the option runs out, because they'd never get it together. I told them, "listen, that's a risk. Because my fear is, they *will* get it together. They *will* make some low-budget piece of shit, and they'll fuck it up, and they'll doit, they'll do it, they'll *turn* the cameras on, on January 5th, no matter what. Starring *whoever*. Because they don't care." I said, "the only way we can win this, is from within. And I need you guys. I don't know what else to tell you, but if you don't do it…that's where we'll be at." I said my piece. Flew back to LA. Then, finally, Rhino is like, "WE'RE GOING TO TELL JOHNNY HE HAS TWENTY FOUR HOURS TO DECIDE IF HE IS DOING THIS MOVIE!" I said, *"you're not going to tell Johnny anything.* Now let me talk to him, okay?" I called Johnny, and told him that they were breathing down my neck, that I had to give them an answer. "What do you think? Can we meet up…" I went through this whole entire day, of Johnny calling me, every couple hours, freaking out, trying to decide. He had to *decide*!

LL: Because he *wanted* to do the film, but he probably wanted to do it right, right from the beginning! It was obviously something about-

LN: No, he wasn't opposed to Alex Cox, necessarily. Of course, he didn't *know* what I knew, but that being said, maybe with Johnny, Alex would have been okay. I don't know.

GG: Do you want me to move that pillow?

LN: Yes, it's too big. So, this *whole day of hell* goes on, while I am waiting by the phone. Johnny's lawyer didn't want him to do it. His *agent* didn't want him to do it. And finally I said to him, "Johnny, I'll just tell you one thing. I can't promise you that it's going to be easy. I can't promise you that you'll get paid much of anything." Of course, Rhino was offering him no money. I said, "I can't promise anything, but I can promise you *one thing*: if you don't do it…*you'll regret it for the rest of your life*." About six p.m., he calls me. He says, "I'm gonna go talk to my agent. And then I'm going to come and see you and tell you what my decision is."

GG: *Gonna go talk to the agent*. Ha ha ha! They are never seen again, when they say that…

LN: I hang up the phone and say, "well, I'm FUCKED." Right? Six o'clock. Seven o'clock. Eight o'clock. Nine o'clock. By now, I'm watching *Star Wars* on TV.

GG: (laughing)

LN: I'm resigned to thinking "if it's meant to be then it's meant to be. If it's not, it's not. I gave it my best shot." But if it didn't happen, I *knew* that my goose was cooked. I knew without Johnny, I was fucked, with the whole Alex Cox thing. So finally, Johnny calls and he says, "where do you live?" I told him, "right around the corner from Canter's." He says, *"oh, well let's go to the Kabitz Room.* I'll meet you there in twenty minutes." I had these books that Ralph Steadman had autographed. He met Johnny, so of course, he was in love with Johnny. And so he sent me all these books with his autograph in them, for Johnny. I thought, "well, I'll take him the books." I'm walking over there, thinking, "at least he's a good guy. He's going to tell me in person." So we're sitting there. I'm *avoiding the topic*. I'm thinking, once the topic comes up, and it's gonna be "no", *the evening's over*!

LL: (laughing)

LN: I *might as well* enjoy my last moments. I give him the books. And finally, Johnny says, "OH! I have something to tell you!" I swivel around on my bar stool, braced for the bad news. "Yeah?" Johnny says, "Let's do it!" "What?" "Let's do it." I spontaneously LEAPT off the barstool, threw my arms around Johnny, and it was like Christmas and New Years, in *one night*. That was probably one of the best nights I ever had, regarding *Fear & Loathing*. We had so much fun. We were laughing. He says, "I only have three conditions. One, I want my money in a brown paper bag. Secondly, we can't start in January. We have to push it." Which was *music* to my ears, right? "THIRD, Steve Nemeth has to come to the set, every day, and pull down his pants, so I can beat his *ass* with a wire hanger in front of the cast and crew." So I said, "fine! You got it!" Meanwhile, everyone's waiting for my call. But I didn't call anyone that night. We went out, we went to the Viper Room. I'm dancing at the Viper Room. Johnny's there, and he's going, "oh shit." We're out till four in the morning, and I was *so* happy. Then, I get up at nine, and call Steve Nemeth. "Okay. Johnny's gonna do it. But these are the conditions." Blah, blah, blah. "And third, you have to take your pants down, on the set, every day." He says, "Okay. Fine!"

[Everyone laughs]

LN: There was a meeting at eleven o'clock with a costume designer and Alex in the production offices.

GG: Just a second...was Johnny in *Hunter-mode* that night?

LN: No. He was just being Johnny. *But*...he'd been hanging out with Hunter a little bit. He knew what the drill was.

LL: *That's* dedication.

LN: I adore him, because he's a person who *really does things* out of commitment and passion. He said to me, "nobody wants me to do this." We had had this conversation. He said, "they didn't want me to have the Viper Room either." And I said, "well, what happens when nobody wants you to do it?" He said, "then I wanna do it!" I said, "well, maybe it's a good sign that they don't want you to do *Fear & Loathing.*"

LL: ALRIGHT, SO HOW DID YOU GET RID OF FUCKIN COX?

GG: Oh Jesus.

LL: We all think Johnny Depp is adorable. We'd ALL let him whip our asses with coat hangers.

GG: *Christ*!

LL: But we *know* that he's the one that wants it.

GG: (sighs)

LN: He's a *doll*. Nobody has a right to look that good, even at 6 AM on a set. Well, about Alex, I didn't care. The power had shifted. And if Alex wants to be the director, he's gonna have to shape up. It's a new ball game! I felt okay about it, I was willing to try. I'm on my way to meet Alex, and I get a call from Johnny. And he says, "yeah…I *just got this weird call from Alex*." Usually a director will call and say, "GREAT!" You'd think Alex would be happy that we got Johnny Depp! And we'd wanted Benicio DelToro already. I knew about Benicio when I was working with Jake Scott. At the time, I thought he might be too young, but I'd been thinking about him. So he was already hanging around. And Johnny was okay with that. Anyway, I go in to meet with Alex, and I'm extremely happy. Apparently, what he had said to Johnny was, "WELL, *WE'RE* READY TO GO! We're ready to go in *January*!" And Johnny was like, "well, I'm *not* ready to go. But I *am* gonna do it." Alex just wasn't happy, I guess. I walk into the meeting. Some poor costume woman was there. Alex was just *spitting tacks*. But I'm in such a good mood. *Nothing* could rain on my parade that day. And the costume woman says, "oh yeah, I heard Depp is going to do the movie." And Alex just hisses, *"he's NEVER going to do the movie*! He says he's going to do it, but he won't be finished with what he's doing!" I said, "well Alex, I think if he said he's gonna do it, he's gonna do it. I'm not worried about *that*." Christmas time rolls around. We have a break. During the break, I get a call from Hunter. "This guy, Alex Cox, wants to come out to Woody Creek." Alex had called Hunter on his own, and made a plan to go out and visit Hunter with his girlfriend, who was the co-writer of the so-called script.

GG: I can only imagine that it didn't go down very well.

LN: It…was…a…*DISASTER.*

GG: Heh HAH!

LN: And the best part is that we have a tape of it. Hunter taped *the whole thing*, which is a tape I'd like to donate eventually, to UCLA.

GG: A *video* tape?

LN: Uh huh! It should be titled, "How NOT To Approach A Writer When You Want To Adapt Their Book." So when Hunter found out about the animation sequence, in this meeting, he was pissed. And Hunter, I have to say, he behaved *so well*. He welcomed them and everything. Alex just hangs *himself*. I'd never called Alex an asshole to Hunter. Before Alex went there, I never said anything negative about him to Hunter. All Hunter said to me was, "why aren't *you* coming?" Hunter had told me that when he asked Alex why I wasn't coming, Alex said "no, that wouldn't be productive." I said to that, "you see what *you* think of him. He's a smart guy, you might like him. Just read the script." Hunter started reading parts of it, and I pointed out to him, "here's where I have a problem with it!"

GG: The animation part. You described it before but my tape machine wasn't functioning. Could you repeat just a few details about that?

LN: Well, I didn't even *tell him* about the animation.

LL: But the condensing of the two major speeches…

LN: Okay, *that* I told him. And that whole middle section, I told Hunter that I had a problem with that. And I didn't even bring up the animation because I *knew* he'd just fuckin FLIP. It was an animated sequence of Hunter on a wave of *bones*, a little animated Hunter, being washed *back* to Las Vegas. Or something like that.

[Awkward pause. Then everyone starts laughing.]

LN: Anyway, it's all on this videotape. Hunter starts looking at this script. Then he *comes up on the animation sequence*, and he reads it. "What the fuck is THIS? Huh? What do you mean, *animation*?" So they get into an argument, and Alex stupidly says, "wellll… you have cartoons in your book. What about *Ralph Steadman*, see here? You have…" And Hunter says, "yeah, they're *illustrations*! They're not fuckin ANIMATION! They're not *CARTOONS*! I don't want *CARTOONS* in my movie!" (giggles) And Alex says, "oh, I suppose when you were a little boy, you *didn't like cartoons*." Hunter says, "NO! I fuckin hated cartoons!" (laughs) This goes on and on. It goes from bad to worse. The more Alex tries to go mano-a-mano with Hunter, the worse it gets. And I can see, knowing Hunter, that he's being polite, but one, two, three, it's starting to build now, and he's *really* getting pissed off. He loses it. He goes after Alex. He says, "who the FUCK said you could do this in the script?" And so Alex says, "*the producer!*" (long pause) "LAILA said I could do it!" *He blames me*! And Hunter says, "we'll see about that." And he starts dialing my number! Whereupon, *Alex leaves*! He runs away!

LL: Busted in his own noose.

LN: The next day, Alex called Steve Nemeth at Rhino. He says he had a *wonderful* meeting with Hunter. Meanwhile, Hunter is calling *me*, going "THAT FUCKIN SLIMY ASSHOLE! I won't have *anything* to do with him. Ever!" I'm going, "oh SHIT." Right? But I'm also exuberant, because Hunter is on my side now, and it always works out better that way. But I didn't do it! I didn't pull a Macchiavellian maneuver. I just let this fuckin guy keep being himself and keep hanging himself. So of course, Johnny knows all about this. But Johnny, to his credit, does not want to be the kind of actor who comes onto a project and *fires a director*. Johnny was very loyal to Alex…beyond the call of duty. He was always saying, "I think we can work it out, let's try to work it out", *et cetera*. We decided we'd have a reading of Alex's script, *with* Johnny and Benicio. Meanwhile, Benicio and I have now become tight, because we're talking a lot. A lot of time is going by. We're hanging out and going through the script, page by page. We're sort of writing our own version of the script, to put back in what we want, to make it how we think it should be. I'm spending *hours* with Benicio, doing this. He gets so into everything and is so committed.That's the way he prepares for a role. He gets so *into* everything, and so committed. I got all these great actors then, to come and do the reading. Rhino is there. And suddenly it's me, Johnny, and Benicio, sitting on one side, and Alex on the other. And I think Alex may have noticed right there, like, "uh oh! When did Benicio become a traitor?" We do the reading…and there *are* things that are funny, in the reading. And when you *see* Johnny and Benicio together finally, you *get it*! There wasn't anything in the script that wasn't going to be there anyway, it was all stuff from the book. Then we get to the wave speech and all that crap that's going on. We finish the reading and everybody leaves, except for me, Johnny, Benicio, and Alex. So the guys try to *talk to him* about it! And he does *not* want to hear it. He's furious. He doesn't wanna deal with it. He's really defensive. Johnny and I leave. Johnny, Benicio and I are standing outside. Johnny says, "you know what? Maybe Benicio and I should talk to Alex. *Ourselves*. He obviously has a hard on *for you*." I said, "yeah, okay. You guys try." So they take Alex to the Viper Room one night, and they beat on him for a while, but they *really* talked to him. They said, "you gotta do this and you gotta do that. *This* is what we all want." I don't know what was *actually* said, but something along those lines. But what ultimately happened, was that Alex said "alright...I'm going to take a week. I'm going to do a re-write. If you don't like it after that-I've taken your notes-I will leave the project." Now I'm thinking, he's gonna change it! All he has to do is change the shit, and he's still in! That's the deal! Why wouldn't he?

GG: Well of course! That's what he said!

LN: No, he said, "I'm gonna do a re-write and if you don't like it…"

GG: Then he didn't actually *say* he would cut the animation sequence?

LN: He *knew* the animation had to go. I'm pretty sure that ultimately, he *did* take the cartoon out. Lydia! You have to hear this, because you're going to like my-

[Note: A deafening clatter of plates and dishes roars out of the kitchen door. -ed]

LL: I'm listening. I've got a knife in my hand, so I'm listening.

LN: I get so riled up with this story.

TAPE CUTS

GG: I knew a lot of ugly shit went down-

LN: A LOT of shit went down.

GG: Yeah, but I never really heard too many of the details. A lot of this stuff has never come out until now.

LN: Well, thank god he never got to the set. Because I can only imagine what he'd be like on a set! He kept talking about *masters*. He kept saying, "I like to do things in *masters*." Masters are like long shots. And I'm thinking, "*this movie's not about masters*! There's a lot of really close-up shit going on. Don't you want to get into the *characters*?"

GG: Alex Cox likes to mock his own stories, as he tells them, it seems. And that's worked for some of his films, that has a lot to do with his sense of humor.

LN: Yeah. Well anyway, Cox goes off to do his re-write. *Meanwhile*, I call Hunter. By now, Hunter and I are *fabulously* in cahoots, because there's nothing better than to-

GG: -have a common enemy.

LN: Yes. To have a common enemy, and to strategize, and just to have Hunter on your side. Of course, Johnny wants Hunter to be happy. And Johnny knows that Hunter is *really* not happy. So I call Hunter and tell him about the re-write. When you get the re-write in a week, if there's any chance he does what they say, great, but whatever happens, you'd better be here. Right? You better get here...and *bring the tape*! (laughs) I threw a big dinner party. Hunter came. He brought the tape. We watched the tape the night before the party, at Johnny's place. And then...everybody got to see what this guy was really like. He's not behaving that way to Johnny, really. The next day we were getting the script back, and that night I had organized the big party for Hunter. I invited people he wanted to see, like Harry Dean [Stanton] and others. Johnny, Benicio, and the agents, *and* the lawyers, the whole crowd. I invited Steve Nemeth and the head of Rhino. Everybody *except* Alex. I figured, "*fuck him*! I don't have to invite him to *anything*!" The day of the dinner party, I got the script. I looked at it. (pause) He didn't change anything. It was like a *"fuck you."* Also, I found out that during that week, he had called Steve Nemeth, and said, "listen, I'm going to do this re-write and everything, but…either I go or Laila goes."

GG: His career was hurting at that point anyway! He wasn't really doing well enough to call a shot like that was he?

LN: But WHY? What had I *done*? If he only knew how much I could have done! But I just let him hang himself. I *could* have really worked hard against him, but I was thinking, "fuck! If I'm stuck with it I'm stuck with it."

LL: Okay, *dinner party*. Let's skip to the annihilation of Alex Cox.

LN: Okay, the dinner party. We're waiting for Johnny to arrive. *I've seen the script.* I know that he hasn't changed anything. I've *told* Hunter. The general attitude towards Cox is "fuck him". But we're waiting for Johnny. We haven't heard what Johnny thinks. He arrives, looks at the script, and just says, "the fucker". At one point, Benicio was talking to Steve Nemeth, and he said, "I don't know. It doesn't look good for Alex." And Johnny's agent leans in, and says *"Alex Cox, bye bye!"* Now, Alex tried to *sue* Rhino, and this is where I have to be careful saying that we fired him. We did *not* fire him. He *said*, "if you don't like what I do with this, I'll leave." He *also* had thrown down a gauntlet, "it's either Laila or me." We came back to him and said, "creative differences, Alex. You *didn't* do what the guys wanted. We *don't* want to do this script. You've now said you won't change the script. And also, *Laila's not leaving.* So that's it. We're gonna part ways, amicably. He came back trying to sue, saying Rhino fired him. They didn't. He fired *himself.*

TAPE CUTS

LN: So now I have to deal with Johnny's agent, Tracey Jacobs, because now Johnny has approval of director. I didn't know Tracey very well. I eventually became very good friends with her, but she's *very* tough. She's a really great agent and she's great to have on your side. That's because she'll do *anything* for Johnny. We wanted to find a director. I would say, "what about Nic Roeg?" "NO!" I *tried* to bring them Alexander Payne, who had done-
GG: Oh, he's great. He did *Election* and-
LN: Yeah, and the one with Laura Dern, which I love.
GG: Oh yeah, the abortion comedy…
LL: *Citizen Ruth.*
GG & LN: *That's it*!
LN: So I go and talk to Alexander Payne, before he did *Election*, of course. I said, "I would love for you to do *Fear & Loathing*!" I think he is so brilliant. I brought him to Rhino…and he *wasn't big enough for them*! I was just shaking my head. It was *that* kind of shit, all the time. I'm very good at spotting talent. Knowing who's going to be good, knowing who's going to be great. The

problem was convincing *other people* at the time. I'm always *ahead* of it.

GG: Alexander Payne has a mean, hateful sense of humor that would have been perfect for *Fear & Loathing*.

LN: He would have been perfect! He would have been great!

LL: So how do we arrive at Tery Gilliam, then?

LN: *And* he's good looking, you know? So not just guts, *maybe sex*!

GG: (laughs)

LN: I'm always thinking. *And* guts! Not enough sex, that's what I'm coming to. There's a *whole* lotta guts, but *not enough fuckin sex*!

GG: That seems to have been a recurring complaint with the magazine.

LL: That's why we've updated the website. *Okay*! So how did you come to Terry?

GG: Who else was being considered?

LN: Oooh, lots. There was Tony Scott, and a lot of others, a lot of names were thrown out. But a lot of people who were unavailable at the time. We were working on a short schedule.

GG: I thought Gilliam was busy too, and that's why the film was shot so incredibly quickly.

LN: Yeah. Ironically enough, I got a fax from Gilliam ten years before, because I had sent him the script. Also because Ralph Steadman is friends with him. He wrote me back, saying "I'm sorry, I can't do it." In pre-production, I stuck that up on my bulletin board, like "ha ha, little did you know..." Gilliam came in from Rick Yorn, but he also came in though Ralph Steadman too, because Ralph had always championed Terry for the movie. Rick York, Benicio's manager met with Terry Gilliam in London and said, "why don't you do it?" Terry *wanted* to do this movie called *The Defective Detective*, which was in the middle of being set up. I called Terry up. He knew who I was, because I had contacted him before. I said, "listen, why don't you just do it? We've *got* Johnny Depp. It's all ready to go. He said, "I *really* wanna do this other movie, but I'll know in a week." I kept hearing that it wouldn't happen, but he was hoping that it would. I said, "well, so now you know there's *one* person in LA who hopes it *doesn't happen*." He said, "well…what does *that* say about our working relationship?" I said, "well, I just think you should do *Fear & Loathing* first, and *then* do *Defective Detective*. It's ready to go!" So, *Defective Detective did* fall apart. We talked him into coming to meet with us. Hunter came back again and we all met with Terry. Terry brought his producer, Patrick Cassavettes, who I liked, even though he's like the English Army.

TAPE CUTS

LN: It's a legendary, insane, crazy book, a seminal book of a certain time. In a lot of ways, Terry fit right in. It takes that kind of insanity. And also to jump in to the chaos that had already been created…and the deals that were still not *totally* in place. Of course, as soon as Terry got involved, the budget doubled. We had half of it from some Rhino foreign sales, and Universal did a negative pickup for the other half. I was happy, because now it was an eighteen million dollar budget and I could hopefully do the things I wanted to do with it. Terry agreed to do it. The one thing that I can say about Terry, is that he *did* get that fire in him about making it happen. It *took* that commitment. Johnny had that. Benicio had it. I had it. And Terry had it. *Nobody else* would have put up with the shenanigans that went on to *get* it finally moving, and done. As we were doing it, with all the insanity, anybody else would have just said, "oh *fuck* this! It's too hard." Of course, I'd still like to stick a fork in his eye, but he'd probably *like it*.

TAPE CUTS

LN: I have to tell this story, it's the funniest part. We're in pre-production with Terry Gilliam. We're back in the same offices we were using with Alex Cox. But, as opposed to those days, working with Cox, when all the doors were closed, now all the doors are open. Everybody's working. Terry's great in pre-production because he's very open. The deals haven't been done. We are still facing another option agreement with Rhino running out. Rhino is getting nervous that they're gonna lose the rights. Rhino, in all their infinite wisdom, allow Steve Nemeth's brilliant power play. He sends me a letter, it comes through to my office. And it says, "well, since the deal hasn't been done, and we *are* facing a deadline, and we *don't know* if this deal *will* be done, we are now concurrently prepping a lower budgeted version of *Fear & Loathing*, to be directed by Alex Cox."

[Room explodes with laughter.]

LN: "Of course, this isn't our *first* choice, but be feel we need to do this. Would you please ask Johnny and Benicio if they would be prepared to stay on, in this new version…or could you give us a list of other potential actors."

LL: Are they insane?

LN: YEAH. *We're in pre-production*! Terry's in the office next door to me! Johnny's about to *shave his head*! We're on a roll! But the deals haven't been done! This is what happens, you know. There's a lot of machinations involved with doing these deals. Rhino was afraid that they were gonna get *cut out*. I don't know what they were really afraid of, because it was all going to be fine. First of all, when you have one director working on something, it's *illegal* to hire another director. I had this horrifying vision of a sweatshop ghetto production office with Alex toiling away on the other side of town, doing *his version* of the film.

GG: *The EVIL Fear & Loathing*!

LN: Yeah! His version of *Fear & Loathing* being concurrently prepped, so that when this deal fell apart, things would just shift across town to the sweatshop.

GG: The inner-film-studio-tabloid demons. Evil machinery.

LN: And of course, that letter was like a red flag to a bull. I go, "WHAT? What is he thinking?" I happily faxed a copy of this to *everybody*. Johnny's agent, the lawyers, Hunter. Everybody.

To all the agents and lawyers who were working round the clock to figure out this complicated dealmaking. And…the shit hit the fan. I mean, the shit *really* hit the fan. And it was so much fun, I can't tell you. Johnny actually called Steve Nemeth, and read him the Riot Act.

TAPE CUTS

GG: I think we're rolling.

LN: So Johnny called Steve Nemeth, and there are things I can't repeat that he said, actually. Everybody just went fucking apeshit when they found out what was going on, and so it backfired in Steve Nemeths' face. About a week later Steve was slinking into the office with these bad *Fear and Loathing* hats that they'd made. He was giving them to people. And he comes into my office and goes, "You gotta help me with Johnny!" Johnny had said, "If you show up on the set, I'm gonna beat the shit out of you." (laughing) He was basically banned from the set, and Terry didn't want to have anything to do with him anymore. At one point, Steve ran into Terry. And Terry said, "Every film needs a scapegoat - and you're it".
GG: (laughs)
LN: "Get out of my way, I got a movie to make." So Steve comes into my office. He says, "you gotta help me with Johnny." And I said, "I can't help you - you dug your own fucking grave. I don't control Johnny! What were you thinking? And not only that, what about me? You're

writing me a letter telling me I'm gonna have to work with Alex Cox again?" (laughs)

GG: (laughs)

LN: I said, "How's that gonna work exactly? In what universe was that happening?" And Steve said, "well, we had to do *something*!" I said, "You just did the one thing that guaranteed that you are not going be on the set and you will not be part of this movie. And there's nothing I can do about it. I can't cover for you. I can't tell the guys - they've already made up their minds." So Steve Nemeth was never on the set, and was never part of the making of this movie. He goes around to colleges and talks about how he "produced" *Fear and Loathing in Las Vegas*. In my contract and in the deal I negotiated with Steve, I was supposed to be the sole producer. Rhino was going to be executive producers. And I had a baggage clause that if a director or a star brought a producer that had to be part of the deal to get the deal *done*, I would make way for one other producer, and *only* one. Well that's what happened. Terry brought his line producer, Patrick Cassavettes. That was fine with me because he's a line producer, and I needed a line producer. That was part of the deal, he came with Terry anyway. So I said "*fine,* it will be me and then Patrick." Soon after, I got a call from the lawyers. "No, Steve Nemeth is the other producer. There has to be three." And I shouted back, "Absolutely not!" I had to fight with lawyers all the way through the making of the movie up until the credits being put on the movie. And finally, Universal said, "Since you guys can't settle it, we're just going to give him the credit." I think they figured Rhino could battle with lawyers longer than I could. It was really shitty. And *nobody* stuck up for me. I even had Terry's people and Johnny's people saying, "Oh well, you know, you're lucky to have a movie made, why don't you just give him the credit?" I said, "You know what? It's the principal of the thing. If he'd done anything - if he'd worked on it - but not only that, he *knows* what we discussed, he knows what the deal was. And I've lived up to my part of the deal."

GG: You've spent like almost 20 years at this point...

LN: Yeah. They said to me, "be the bigger person." I said, "why don't you tell *him* to be the bigger person? Why do I have to be the bigger person? I'm the one doing the job!"

There's no producers union. People shouldn't get credit for things they didn't do. And in the end, the way they made it up to me was they gave me my production credit. "A Laila Nabulsi Production." Which did soften the blow. That's a good credit for me to have, and it does say that was my production. But it didn't change how I feel, morally, about how people act, and how I feel about the way people will just stab you in the back out of ego. It's one of those resentments. I have a *few* that come to haunt me - and I try to process them and let them go, constantly. And every once in a while they pop back up. In fact, when I was thinking about doing this interview for Sex & Guts, I woke up a couple times in the night, thinking "and *THEN*..."

GG: (laughs)

LN: "…so-and-so did THIS to me, and this one did that, and then they did this…"

GG: We can still go there if you want….

LN: Yeah, but in the end, *Fear and Loathing in Las Vegas* was a big piece of art that we threw up on to the big screen. And it was Gonzo filmmaking. I've *heard* that Terry said that he thought we were "all in over our heads", and I really don't agree with that. Maybe *he* was. He decided to do it in a year, completely, and he did himself a disservice. He rushed through the editing. I also think he missed some of what *Fear and Loathing* was really about. Terry Gilliam wants to be the genius on the set, and the truth is that the genius was the *piece*, and Hunter's piece. It's the macho attitude. "Well no, *I'm* the genius".

GG: "I've done this and I…."

LN: Almost saying, "fuck Hunter." There was that strange sense of competition. Well, there shouldn't have been. This was a love letter. Our purpose as a whole was to *serve the piece.*

GG: You don't think the movie does that? What's your feeling on the finished product?

LN: I saw it recently. It was on TV a couple months ago. I hadn't seen it in awhile. And I thought, "wow, it's really funny and it works. It's good!" As time goes by, there are still things that will haunt me. For example, I think he fucked up the revolving bar scene…

GG: Yeah, right, it's like too… slapstick in a way.

LN: Yeah, it's too slapstick, and it's Terry's kind of humor. Which is not my kind of humor, ultimately. He's very broad. And I don't feel he's a real actor's director. He likes the sets and the props.

GG: You can really tell that in the movie. But there was depth to the characters.

LL: Fortunately the actors that were chosen were superlative.

LN: Yeah, and thank God for Benicio. Because, Benicio is not necessarily a comedic actor. I'm sure he can do it if he wants…

LL: And it's such non-ego driven performances. That's the beauty of that film. The level of dedication to the material just shines through.

LN: Yeah, it does shine through. And I have to say that Johnny *was* great and he has so much more soul than people realize. I mean, both Hunter and Johnny are from Kentucky. When I went to meet Johnny, when we first talked about him doing it, I thought, "well, he's not physically as big as Hunter." And I always thought of the guys in the book as the *double threat*. They're both very tall and big and…you see 'em both coming.

GG: (laughs)

LN: But when I met with Johnny, he has the same eyes as Hunter. He has those darkbrown, vulnerable eyes. And he's got that Southern gentleman quality that Hunter has. And I thought, "wait a minute, he's got that quality that people don't necessarily associate with Hunter." I was sure that he could do all the other stuff, but it was always that *thing* I was looking for. That being the certain quality that makes you realize that there's this intelligence here, there's this sensitivity here, in the character. A sensitivity that you only know if you know Hunter. I saw that suddenly in Johnny's eyes. I remember asking Johnny, the first time I met him: "you're not as tall as Hunter. Does that bother you?" And he said, "I can do it." And I thought, "wait a minute. Johnny Depp is telling me he can do it,so I'm sure he can do it. What am I complaining about?" But I really was convinced when I met with him, because he had that *thing* that Hunter has.

And then *Benicio*. In the movie, the Hunter character really is the *mind* of the piece and the Gonzo character is the *soul* of the piece. It's the soul of the 60s. What Gonzo really represents is living in the moment. The passion and the dedication for the truth, the unpredictability, and at the same time, it's like one of those flames that's burning so bright that you *know* it's going to die. You know it's going to burn out. Just like the 60s. That's what the whole book is about. Going back again to the *wave speech*…

GG: Exactly.

LN: You know its time has come. They're right at that end, and they know it's all over.

GG: "You can still see the high watermark where the wave broke and rolled back."

LN: Yes!

LL: What's amazing about Hunter S. Thompson being still alive today…is that so many people that have that flame, that intensity and that spontaneity-

LN: -have died.

LL: -have died. Because…

GG: A lot of them never got the big picture the way he does. In some abstract way, I think seeing the big picture, so clearly, has a lot to do with living through something. There is a greater logic, and a greater understanding of the world in his work.

LN: I think also it's just his destiny. He never thought he was going to live, either. So it's funny. I like to think of him as a tantric master. He's an incredible reincarnate. There's something going on there that's meant to be here. Thank God, because I'd hate to think of the day when he's not here. He'll probably outlive me, at this point. You had asked me before, about who I'd considered for casting. Dan Aykroyd and Belushi, before the Blues Brothers incarnation. Belushi *was* actually Gonzo. He *had* that charisma, he had the physicality. He *was* that flame that was burning so bright that you were drawn right to it. He had that warmth.

GG: No regard for social conduct. (laughs)

LN: That's right! No regard for social conduct!

GG: (laughs)

LN: But a sense of the truth, a sense of being a good-hearted person. Not just to fuck with people…

GG: Even when he threw a plate across the room, there was something *right* and *good* in that.

LN: Well it's the pain. It's the *pain* of Gonzo, the pain of Oscar Acosta, the Brown Buffalo, who the Gonzo character was based on. It is the pain of somebody who sees injustice. And that's what the *core* of Fear and Loathing was to me. Here are two people who see the *pain*, and the *fear* and the *loathing* of the American dream getting sucked into hell by the cops, by the consumerism, by the powers that be.

GG: If you feel that pain that acutely, you're forced to embody it somehow. It doesn't remain trapped inside, you can't keep it there. In *Fear and Loathing In Las* Vegas, they lived it. It was in their minds *all the time*.

LN: Oscar Acosta was a Chicano Rights lawyer here in LA. He was doing incredible things. He was was burning judges' lawns and staging all kinds of events for Brown Power. He had been a missionary and had worked in a leper colony. This was a guy who was wildly bigger than life-

GG: -while projectile vomiting blood off his back porch. A twisted saint, a hero.

LN: Right, all those things combined. He used to talk about the Bible and God, and then he'd go off into "walking with the king." That's what he called doing acid.

GG: Yeah, I read his book, which was great.

LN: Yeah, **The Autobiography of A Brown Buffalo**. But *who could be that guy*? I always thought somebody like Belushi or Brando, *that kind* of bigger than life person. Well along comes Benicio, who looks the part. He had to gain 50lbs, but he has the ethnic background, and he has that pain, that *tortured* pain. What he didn't necessarily have was the comic sensibility of a Belushi. He's not necessarily an improv type. He's a method actor. What was great about him in the film ultimately, was that he held down that *reality center*. As if to say, "this isn't fun and fucking games. *This is my life*." And whatever's going on is going on but it's not necessarily "ho ho ho!", right? He's *serious*. When he's in the bathtub trying to kill himself, he was *trying to kill himself*. The comedy of that is in how serious he truly is. So Benicio understood that he had to really play it for real. This is a guy who…okay, look. Oscar Acosta would burn himself with cigarettes. He had those burn marks. Benicio *actually burned himself with cigarettes*. He didn't put make-up cigarette burns on his arm. And they weren't necessarily even seen! You can see them if you look, in the movie, but nobody made a big deal of it. I think at one point we were going to show him actually *doing* it. I don't remember what happened, we ended up not shooting that. But, he DID it. I was worried, these burns looked infected at one point. And I said, "are you sure you're cleaning those?" The nurse had looked at it. He hurt his finger one day on the set, so we had to take him to the hospital. We get to the hospital and I'm waiting with him. They made his eyes look bloodshot for the film and his hair is wild.

[LL and GG laugh]

LN: He's 50 pounds overweight. He looks like an insane maniac. He's got a broken finger and all these cigarette burns. So I'm looking at his arm and I see this red line going up his arm…which means blood poisoning. If that gets to your heart, you're dead. And I didn't want to freak him out. Benicio had never seen this before. So I go and grab the doctors and of course they start freaking out. And we told the doctor that he was an actor. But the doctor's not too sure about this *at all*. It's in the middle of the night, and I'm the only one there with him. So the doctor says, "Is there something you're not telling me?" He obviously didn't recognize Benicio and here's this insane fat guy with cigarette burns, a broken finger, and blood poisoning. It was a fucking *trip*. But I gotta say that his commitment and his dedication to that core essence, is what saved it for me. Johnny's great, he's like watching a porpoise swim in the water, he's so easy. And he can change on a dime - he's perfect for Terry in that way. Benicio wasn't. Benicio didn't-

GG: He didn't have the kind of direction that he needed.

LN: Right, and Terry was not supportive to him and did not understand his process. Terry didn't encourage him, and he was exasperated with him most of the time. So the set was kind of like, *East of Eden*. You had the good son that dad liked and you had the bad son that was fuckin James Dean. Benicio and I, in a funny way, became compadres by enduring together the pain of the things we thought weren't going right. Terry and Johnny were happily playing in their world. Johnny did stick up for a lot of things. But in the end Terry has final cut, and he's a bit of a *monster* on the set. So he does it his way. Oh, we *had* a lot of fights. I thought at the time, "You have to pick your battles"…because you can't fight with your director every day. I tried to pick my battles, and there were some things I had to let go of. Like the scene in the bathtub. Hunter throws the grapefruit in the bathtub, so Gonzo really thinks he's being electrocuted. *That*'s the comedy of the moment. Well, Terry thinks it's a funny idea to throw the grapefruit at his head...

GG: Which doesn't work.

LN: Which doesn't work!

GG: No - I noticed that, too.

LN: And I argued about it and it's sort of like I'm a pain in the ass right? And I know it's not gonna work, and I couldn't get him to shoot it the way it's described in the book. And there was one other instance with the desk clerk. The clerk says, "I've been fucked around by a lot of mean-tempered, rule-crazy cops in my time". To the cop, right? So, suddenly I'm on the set and I hear the guy saying, "I've been fucked around by a lot of mean-tempered, rule-crazy *assholes* in my time." And I go, "assholes? Wait a minute. Now... Terry's "writer", hah hah, who helped him work on the script, was Tony Grisoni. This guy from England who didn't have a *fucking clue about anything*. He was on the set for one week, so he changed it on the set. You know, this is what people do, they think they have to make themselves...

GG: "Oh that was me! That was *my* idea."

LN: Yeah! "I was on the set and thank God I did that." I go up to him and I ask, "why are they changing that?" And he says, "it's funnier." *"NO, it's not FUNNIER*!" So I go up to Terry. This is it, when you're shooting, you shoot the scene, you move on. That's the thing about film. It's my life, this crusade I have. And here are the moments that are happening. It's like, "Oh fuck!" It seems like a small thing but... it becomes so important to you. So I go up to Terry. "Why are they saying 'asshole'?" And he goes, "It's funnier." And I go, "But it's *not* funnier." And he starts *screaming*. "WHY? WHY? TELL ME WHY!" And I said, "OK, I'll tell you why. Because the whole point is, it's a *cop*. We're at a *cop* convention. This guy gets to talk for all of us and he gets to tell him, 'fuck you, cop'! There's plenty of assholes in the world that you could work out on-

GG: But this is a COP!

LN: This is about getting to work out on a fucking *cop*. He gets to say to him, "I've been fucked around by cops and I'm gonna fuck *you* around." Right? Then Terry, to his credit, says, "alright, well, we'll shoot it both ways." So I thought, "OK, well that's the best I can do." And my version got in the movie.

GG: Right, but whereas the grapefruit scene remained misunderstood and mis-shot.

LN: Yeah. The grapefruit, even though I thought about it, at that point it was just like...

GG: It doesn't work. The reason he freaks out is that he thinks the grapefruit is actually a radio plunked into the water...

LN: Right.

GG: But it hit him in the head, and there's a difference between a grapefruit hitting your skull and what would have been presumed to be a metal *radio*.

LN: It doesn't make any sense. And I thought about it and now I look back and I think, "God,

you couldn't fight about everything." What if I had fought *every day*? I would have gotten thrown off the set.

LL: (laughs)

LN: Or somebody gets mad at you. It's all a political thing about keeping it going, but trying to get as much as you can. And Terry told a mutual friend of ours in London, after this was all over, he said, "What was it like working with Laila?" And Terry said, "Well, you know, we did get into it and we had some fights but I have to say, she was usually right." But he never told *me* that! You know what I mean? He never gave me that. And I wish he'd given me that more while we were doing it, I wish he had less insecurity and ego, and allowed me to help him. Because I did know the piece better than anybody. We'd done a play version here, I really knew that thing back and forth and I knew what the comedy beats were.

GG: So what happened in the aftermath of the film in terms of your career and what it did for you?

LN: It did absolutely fucking shit for me!

GG & LL: (laughing)

LN: It was so crazy. We went to Cannes and opened the film festival. I'd seen the film edited. [Terry and I had] been having fights about the editing. He wouldn't put in "Sympathy for the Devil" at the beginning, which broke my heart. Johnny even went to the mat for that, but he wouldn't listen to us. So I get to the screening at Cannes, and I'm sitting there to watch the movie - and he's made *further cuts that we didn't know about*. So I'm sitting there through the movie going, "fuck!" And the whole thing was a fucking nightmare. And I was so devastated because it was hard. And I had no objectivity at that time. We went to the party, and by the end of the night I was so devastated. We'd ended up at the Hotel duCap. I got back to my hotel at 5 a.m. and I was crying in the cab all the way home. I was dressed to the nines with jewels, and I had mascara running down my face. When I get out of the cab, in front of the Carlton Hotel, I tripped on my gown-

LL: Oh *no*!

LN: -and I fell flat on my face at the entrance! These two hotel security guys picked me up and poured me into the elevator. But it was the perfect metaphor. At the beginning of the night, you're walking up the red carpet, proudly escorted by your father in your last moments of hope and expectation of life to come. And at the end of the night, you're flat on your face at the Carlton, and you're in ruins! The next day was full of hideous reviews. We got *run out of town*. And then we came to New York and we had a *good* premiere in New York, although that night also ended badly for me.

GG: It was very well liked in New York.

LN: Yeah, it was well liked. Hunter came to the screening.

LL: The job of producer is like the Godmother. It's a lot of cajoling, baby-sitting, hand holding, favor-pulling, pleading, begging, arguing, screaming...

LN: Right.

LL: Crying!

LN: Right.

LL: And then frustration.

LN: And then, as my friend Michael O'Donoghue said, "they kill you with a thousand cuts." By the time you're done it's not one blow to the heart, you're bleeding from every inch of skin. This is how I felt about Terry. I felt like I had this baby, and then I gave the baby to somebody to baby-sit for a couple months. I came back and the baby's legs are all torn and mangled. And they give you back your baby and somebody says, "well, don't you still love your baby?" And you go, "Yeah, I love my baby...but I wish it's legs were straight." It's like that. I love it and it was a great experience and yes, there will always be things that I must carry with me. I wish I could do it over again. After the NY premiere, I crawled off to my friend Janey Buffett's house. My most generous friend in the world. She gave me her guest host in Long Island. And I literally crawled in there with a rash down my back and thoughts of murder in my head and bad reviews and not good numbers. All of that information was coming in. And I thought, "it's just a fucking movie! What the fuck is the big fucking deal!" Why was this such an incredible crusade for me? For *what*? A fucking piece of celluloid in a big tin? I spend years of my life, my *whole energy*! I don't know if I'd ever feel the same way. It's a passion. I have to say that I've lost... not that I've lost that passion, but I don't know how I'd ever get that passionate about something again. It wasn't just a movie for me, it was an era of time. It was my relationship with Hunter. It was personal, it was my love letter to Hunter. It was sort of a culmination of karmic destiny with Hunter. Breaking up with Hunter was not a happy thing for either one of us, and in a way *Fear and Loathing* was a way for us to stay in each other's lives and have something to focus on, almost as if it were our child. I wanted to celebrate the best things about Hunter. I wanted to show him how much I cared and how much I loved him. And in a way, the best moment was when Hunter saw the film and told me he liked it. Because Johnny, Benicio, and I felt like kids who had been running amok in their parents' house. And until he saw it, we didn't know how he would feel. He really liked it. While I was dressing to go to the wrap party of the movie, Hunter called and said, "I just wanted to tell you I'm really proud of you." Maybe I have a daddy complex but that was *it* for me. That's what I needed. And I also felt like it was the end of an era. My karma with Hunter was done. Whatever happens to him, or if he dies tomorrow or whatever, I'm clean. And there was a huge sense of accomplishment, and also a huge sense of how many years we'd been going around town in Hollywood, meeting everybody in the world talking about *Fear and Loathing*. I felt like such a fucking loser. *Fear and Loathing. Fear and Loathing.*

LL: I think in the end, from the outsiders' point of view, it's an amazing fucking film that really sums up something that no other film has captured. And it succeeds in the end, I think.

Fuck the reviews, fuck the numbers, fuck the hassle. It was almost a two decade long nightmare for you! In the end, I think it really depicts something that no other film has captured about the soul of that era. And not only the soul of that era, the soul of-

GG: -Hunter Thompson.

LL: -of a specific people and a specific intellect. True rebellion in the face of that era.

LN: People say to me, "it's a drug movie." And I always say, "no, it's a political movie." I'm very politically oriented and I'm a true patriot in the sense that I'm half Palestinian so you can imagine that gives me that rebellious side. But as an American, I'm a Daughter of the American Revolution. And I feel that Hunter represents, to me at least, that whole sensibility and that whole time of the world. And I was on the tail end of that. I was a product of that era more than I am of any other era, being a hippie or whatever you want to call it.

GG: What is Daughters of the American Revolution? I'm not familiar with that...

LN: Your ancestors fought in the American Revolution. And we go all the way back to the Mayflower, and so I have one side that's total Americana.

GG: So it's quite literal.

LN: Yeah, I have ancestors that fought in the American Revolution, so to me it represents this standard of justice. And I think Hunter represents that too, of The Truth. He represents the pen that is mightier than the sword. And Oscar Acosta, Gonzo, who used the law to fight injustice. There were people who were really trying to change things and expose the truth and the corruption and the insanity of the American bullshit lie. So in a way, I can't believe they actually let us make the movie. It's really subversive. And its not really about drugs, it's about really going into that world and trying to expose it, and the pain of being in it and knowing the truth. Of seeing the wave crashing.

GG: But it doesn't really preach rebellion so much as it explains the rebellion of that time. So now that it's 20 years later, it's not going to bring about things the way it might have, had it happened 20 years ago. What would be different, what would you have predicted about a hypothetical 1975 release of this film?

LN: Well originally at one point, Scorcese did want to do it with Belushi and Aykroyd. And I think if they had done it, it would have been brilliant, it would have been of that time and it would have had that energy. And it would have probably been very exciting. And you know, I think somebody should have done it then, to be honest with you. After the movie came out and I was staying at Janey Buffets' house, I read **Easy Riders, Raging Bulls**, and it really helped me. During that era of filmmaking, many of those guys made films that weren't appreciated at the time.

GG: Friedkin and people like that...

LN: *Raging Bull* wasn't reviewed well when it came out. But I'm much more attuned to that sensibility of filmmaking and being a renegade. And I always am attracted to anti-heroes. They're outlaws, they're true American heroes. Gilliam is American, but he left. He's an anglophile. And as Hunter always said, "he didn't protest the Vietnam War, he was living in England." You know, he's from California.

GG: That's right, he is American, but he's more into a comic book sensibility than a political agenda. He's more grandiose and absurd, which is only one part of *Fear and Loathing*.

LN: I think making the film was, in a way, for him to redeem the fact that he always felt guilty that he had left the country during a time of all that upheaval. He was an expatriate, so in a way it was his way to address the fact. He's a weird guy, Terry. I would certainly work with him again because I know The Monster now. I wouldn't care as much. *It's just too bad it was my baby*. You know it's hard to let go. It's hard for someone like him to come in and take over when there's someone like me around. Maybe he thought, "I've got to rip it out of their hands and *make it* something." And I'm going, "yeah, OK. Fine. I'm here to serve." And he *did* use me in a lot of ways. And I did get a lot of stuff in there.

GG: Well, what's your favorite scene? I mean, what scene do you think works best in terms of the book?

LN: My favorite scene. Well, I love the scene where Benicio and Johnny are talking in the hallway- which Terry cut. There was more to that scene which I wish was in its entirety. You know when they're talking about getting rid of Lucy? And he's like, "we can give her to the cops, keep her full of acid and they can gang

fuck her and she can make us a lot of money!"
And Benicio's like...

GG: "UNGH! UNGH! That's ugly, man!"

LN: And there's a whole thing after that, which I wanted to keep in, where Benicio comes back and says, "OK". Like, there's no witnesses, he takes over the thing, as if he figures out that this is the right idea. "There's no witnesses and she can't identify us!" Johnny says, "us?" And totally turns it around and takes over which I would not have cut and I like that scene. I like the scene where Benicio is in the hallway looking for the key to get into the room. I like *little* things, things like that. I love the *Adrenachrome* scene actually.

GG: That's great, yeah.

LN: Where Johnny's doing that whole thing and he's...

GG: "Nice tits, man!"

LN: And he's freaking out on the phone with Lucy before that, and all that stuff.

GG: And there's those big devil tits on his back...

LN: Yeah I like the small things.

GG: Heh, heh. So what did you think of *Where the Buffalo Roam*? And you had a great Bill Murray story as well. What was that Captains' name? The boat?

LN: Commander Cody. Yes, we firebombed Commander Cody (laughs) but I don't know if I want to tell that story...

GG: Yeah, it's a long story. What's in your near future?

LN: I'm trying to get a movie financed, which has somehow turned into another saga. I don't know why my fate is to take on the most difficult thing and make it happen, or why they turn into the most difficult thing. But it's a reunion of all the original Saturday Night Live guys and Tom Davis [original SNL writer and player, half of the Franken and Davis team with Al Franken- ed.] wrote it. He's one of the original writers and he's going to be a first time director, directing it. It's going to be a "stoner in the suburbs" kind of thing. It's about a man who's out of time. He's a guy who's stuck in that era, who's living in upstate New York, who was a comedy writer on Saturday Night Live. And who doesn't have a job and isn't really doing that great any more, and all his fancy friends… you know all his old friends are famous movie stars and he's not. And he decides he should reinvent his career and write this script. This is what the movie's about. And if he can get Chevy Chase to say he'll be in it, he can get it produced. So he goes to Chevy. Chevy is the only one who plays himself. He says to Chevy, "will you be in it", and he says, "Sure." And of course at the end, Chevy isn't in it. But that's the kind of premise, and all the guys are going to be in it. I hope it will be the only art movie to come out of that era. As opposed to the Lorne Michaels-

GG: -crap spin-off movies.

LN: -versions of comedy movies that are just sketch comedy shit.

GG: They're the worst films. "It's Pat: The Movie", and "Corky Romano." What is *up* with those stupid movies? (Laughs)

LN: I feel bad for Lorne. He always fancied that he would make something like "The Graduate." And his legacy will be…all those movies. After I made *Fear and Loathing*, I ran into Lorne at Carnegie Hall. It was just insane. He said something about *Fear and Loathing*, and he said, "well, it took you long enough."

LL: Well, better to wait and make one important film than to make 10 that won't even equal their weight in celluloid. Or cellulite, actually. They're like a fat dimple on the face of American cinema.

LN: What I said to him was, "Some of the best things in life are worth waiting for." You always have to have those snappy comebacks. (snaps fingers and laughs) Especially when dealing with the lizards of the world. Fucking lizards.

GG: Yeah, pretty necessary in your business.

LN: Yeah. I just had a dealing with an investor, this Arab investor. And I thought, "Oh great - an Arab investor, one of my people!" And the guy just totally fucked me, dropped out of the deal at the last second. "Dear Motherfucker: Thanks for wasting my time." But that's what happens with people who don't know, who've never financed a movie. They have a lot of money, they want to get into the movie business, but the truth is, they don't really understand-

GG: -what a nightmare it is.

LN: -that you have to keep the forward movement, you have to keep the illusion that you're making it alive. You can't stall on the deal. Witnessed by *Fear and Loathing*, if we'd stalled on the deal, we would have never made the movie. We just kept going.

GG: You had to bluff a lot, too.

LN: That's a producer's *job*, is to keep everybody excited. And there's forward

Movement. (excitedly) "We're *making* it, we're doing it, we're doing it, OK, come on!" And when you're in the independent world, you also have the other nightmare of studios, which can also hang you up. And I seem to be forced and regulated to the independent world anyway.

GG: Do you have a dream project? Is there anything that could be as big to you as *Fear and Loathing* was?

LN: I am going to direct something someday. I've worked on enough movies now and also after *Fear and Loathing* - I know I could do that job. I would love to be in the position to live and die by my own sword.

GG: And you know what to look for now.

LN: And also when you're a producer you have to be in service to the director. That's your job and I understand that and I'm willing to do that. But it would be great to make the choices you want to make and not have to deal with somebody else's ego about it. You know, have my own ego! I think maybe that would be something I could ultimately be passionate about. Actually I've been talking to Lydia about working with me.

LL: More Sex!

LN: More sex! Less Guts.

GG: *Less* sex. GUTS! GUTS! MORE GUTS!

LL: Lotsa guts, where the hell is the sex?

GG: Who cares.

LN: I want the *sex*, I'm tired of the guts. I'll tell you something, being a woman and being a producer you'd think you'd get a lot of sex. The problem is, you're like a man - you're in this power position. It's terrible. And the only people you meet are actors, in show business. All the girls I know say "I'll never date another actor." And then you see them making out with Heath Ledger. Well, who wouldn't? But if you're a producer a lot of times actors look at you as a potential *in*. "Maybe she'll put me in a movie." So there's all that shit going on and it's across the board. You're like, "wait a minute, I just want to be a person." And I'm not complaining, I'm not having a bad time. But it's a funny place because as a woman, you're dealing with a lot of guys a lot of the time, and I have no problem with that, I like working with guys. You just can't let them see you cry. That's my main rule.

GG: One thing I wanted to ask you was about one reason it was so was hard to get *Fear and Loathing* made. It was a really dark film in a lot of ways. Last year, there was *In the Bedroom* and *Monster's Ball*, they both came out. And they were, I think what the industry calls, "crossover films", mainstream/independent films. Do you think this is going to open any doors for you? For any projects, if you were going to do any dark films, is it easier now for that kind of thing?

LN: I think *Fear and Loathing* is a comedy. I like dark comedy and I think in anything I do, even if it's dark, will have elements of humor in it. That's just the way I am, I tend to see things that way. No, I don't think anything particularly opens up opportunities for anything. I don't think anybody knows. I think you have to - as an artist of any kind - you have to have your own vision and go for it, no matter what anybody else says. And if it works, it works, if it doesn't, it doesn't. If you start playing games like, "well they want this, or maybe they'll like this," then I'd just make a movie about a retarded Jewish person and get the Academy Award.

GG: (howling with laughter)

LN: And I'm not interested in doing that. My feeling is that if I relate to something and I get that passion for it then it has to be done for *me.* Then I can put everything behind it. If I don't feel it, it doesn't matter what the material is, I can't work on it. I have to *feel* something. Because I know how hard it is to do it. So unless I get that feeling, fuck it. Who wants to do it? I mean, producing is a shit job in that sense. It's the most thankless job on the planet. Everybody else gets the kudos, everybody else gets the glamour. And you're the one running around doing all that work. Unless you're smart enough to get a hit where you own some of it, and you're making a lot of money. *That's* the only revenge. Making a lot of money. I enjoy collecting people, and that's what I'm good at. That's why I'm good at what I do, because I really love people and meeting new people. And talent - finding new talent - and finding out what people are doing. Putting people together. In that sense what *Fear and Loathing* has given me, is legitimacy. When I tell people I made *Fear and Loathing,* they understand that's what I've done. I'm creative, I obviously have some tenacity. I'm a bit off-center and a little bit renegade. And those are the kinds of people I like. Wes Anderson, for instance. I like those kinds of brains, and I want to work with those kinds of people. The thing is, it's not very romantic to be a producer. It's much more romantic to be a movie star or a director.

GG: Well, the project you were talking to Lydia about - are you going to direct that film?

LN: Yeah, that's something I want to direct. What I want to do is direct something and I want it to be a very personal film. I want it to be very original. I mean, it could be a book, it could be something I've found. But as I go along and as we started talking, and because I'm a woman…it's not that I necessarily want to do a "woman's film". I'm not what you would call a feminist in that way, it doesn't enter my world. But what I want to do is something I can get passionate about, that's original, that's different for me, and would be different for other people - that speaks to me in some way. I could write my own thing and have it be totally original, but I like the idea of somebody else *surprising me…* with things I might not normally think of or do. And bringing that to me - and letting me translate it and put my stuff on it as well - that's more interesting to me. That's why I love adapting books, because somebody's already constructed it. It's hard to write, too. I have a lot of ideas in my head, and scenarios I think about doing.

TAPE CUTS

GG: Oh yeah, and midget pron, for example.

LN: Yeah, Terry's obsessed with midgets, you know. And he always has midgets in his movies. There's *one* in *Fear & Loathing*, at the Polo Lounge. The dwarf, who brings the telephone.

GG: Who we've all seen before in other films.

LN: *That* guy. Yes. And that was sort of it, I thought. But then, these midgets kept *appearing*. They kept showing up as extras, here and there. And I *knew* we were heading towards Circus Circus. I knew it would be a midget-fest. I wasn't overly fond of the idea. I have nothing against midgets, but I was getting nervous about this turning into a Terry Gilliam extravaganza midget-fest.

GG: Right. (laughs)

LN: He *knew* I was freaking out about it. And there was a few days there when they kept coming in for auditions. They were *everywhere*. I was getting more and more upset about it. Then he *did* film this extravaganza at the Circus Circus, in the beginning. All the midgets you see in that scene, that was his idea. That was a *whole new element* that *he* put in. I remember him telling us all his "great idea", and I was thinking, "oh no!"

GG: Veering towards *Brazil 2*!

LN: It was driving me crazy! There wasn't very much I could do about it, but accept it, and say something every once in a while. He *knew* it was driving me crazy. So I had a friend of mine, who shall remain nameless, dig through his extensive porn collection. I called him up and I said, "do you have any *midget porn*?" He said, "actually…yes, I do." I said, "well, can you make a copy?" He came to the set, brought me a couple of copies, *two tapes* of midget porn. I said to Johnny, "guess what I'm going to give Terry today? *Midget porn.*" He jumps up and says, "let's watch it!" So we watch it in the trailer. We were very disappointed, it was only midget women. And Johnny Depp said, "*I want midget DICK!*" But there wasn't any midget dick. Anyway, it was really *awful*. It was the final blow in the whole scenario.

GG: *Everything's going wrong*! Not even the midget porn is right.

LN: I put the tapes in a manilla envelope, and walked over to Terry. "Oh, I have a present for you!" I gave it to him and said, "don't open it till you get home." He took it home…and he *never* said a word to me about it again! I have *no idea* what he thought. I'm sure he was like, "HA. HA. HA." *Or*…maybe he was delighted. I have no idea.

GG: Maybe he was offended and hurt by that gesture.

LN: I have *no idea*.

GG: Because I've noticed, you know, that there is never any sex in Terry Gilliam's films.

LN: (laughing)

GG: So maybe he's just touchy about the whole interpersonal, fluid contact-kind-of-thing.

LN: I *don't know*. I *do* know that it gave *me* a sense of satisfaction. I have no idea what it did to him. My thought was, "okay, you like them so much? Well *here ya go*. You might as well *go for it*."

TAPE CUTS

LN: Somewhere near the end of the shoot, we were shooting on the Universal lot. We were shooting the *maid scene,* in the hotel suite, which is semi-*wrecked*. Not totally wrecked yet. The bond company was getting kind of hot under the collar. Patrick Cassavettes and I were sitting outside, in the hallway, which was done up like part of the set. We're out there in the hall. They're shooting inside. The bond guy comes running up and starts *screaming* at us. "I'M GONNA TAKE OVER THIS PICTURE!" I guess he thought we'd gone overboard, and I don't know why, because logistically we were doing fine. But he seemed to think we weren't. He was *screaming* at us, saying *"THIS PICTURE IS OUT OF CONTROL!"* And at that very moment Johnny *burst* out of the door, right in front of us, wearing that hat, and the lipstick, and the feather in his hat, in a dressing gown. And smiling broadly, he barks out, "HI!"
GG: (laughing)
LN: Then he came over and gave me a kiss, and I thought, "No we're not out of control!" (laughing hysterically) "We're *fine*!"
GG: He looks great in lipstick. Bald Johnny in lipstick, smeared all over-

LN: *-which Hunter likes to do.* That wasn't made up.

GG: I heard a rumor that Hunter physically attacked Johnny at the New York premiere.

LN: That could be *very true*. I don't know. Hunter was *at* the New York premiere. He did come in and watch the movie. He threw a bunch of popcorn at people. Yeah, we had a great time.

GG: I heard that Criterion Classics is doing a new DVD of *Fear & Loathing*.

LN: Yeah, it's going to have a lot of great stuff on it. They found video footage of Oscar Acosta which no one has ever seen. Benicio and Johnny did audio tracks. Hunter is going to do an audio track. I'm going to see Hunter next weekend to do an audio contract. Actually, I happened to catch *Fear & Loathing* on TV recently. I sat there and I laughed all the way through. I thought, in the end, that everybody did a great job. Terry did a great job. It was better than I thought. I am proud of Johnny and Benicio and Terry. It gets better every time I watch it. I think Hunter was right when he called it "an eerie trumpet call over a lot battlefield."

TAPE CUTS

-fin-